Ann Falcone Sha...

15 April 2025
Newport News, VA

Lost and Found

To: Tom & Helen
Jim... is the school in which
we learn.

Wider Perspectives Publishing ¤ 2024 ¤ Hampton Roads, Va.

Ann Falcone Shaleski

The poems and writings in this book are the creations and property of Ann Falcone Shalaski, the author is responsible for them as such. Wider Perspectives Publishing reserves 1st run rights to this material in this form, all rights revert to author upon delivery. Author reserves all rights thereafter: Do not reproduce without permission except Fair Use practices for approved promotion or educational purposes. Author may redistribute, whole or in part, at will, for example submission to anthologies or contests.

Editing assistance provided by Crickyt J. Meier (writes as Crickyt J. Expression).

© 2024, Ann Falcone Shalaski, including writing as Ann Shalaski
1st run complete in December 2024
Wider Perspectives Publishing, Hampton Roads, Va.
ISBN 978-1-964531-03-8

Author's Note

This book is dedicated to you, the reader, and to anyone facing physical challenges and life challenges.

Lost and Found was written with courage, compassion, wisdom and hope, in the aftermath of a stroke and the long journey to recovery.

Every 40 seconds someone suffers a stroke. There are 795,000 strokes a year.

Behavioral changes often include fear, frustration, grief, sadness, anxiety, loss of identity, and mental flooding.

On a More Personal Note

Thank you to all my fellow poets and friends for your support. Without you, the journey would have been lonely, the destination uncertain.

A special thank you to Joanna and Patty for your constant encouragement, advice and joy through the trying times.

To J. Scott Wilson, editor and publisher of Wider Perspectives Publishing. Thank you to C.J. Expression for helping me realize the destination was one small step at a time.

Foreword

Ann Falcone Shalaski, in her collection Lost and Found, graciously allows readers into Secret Places (Pg 33) of her mind, discovered while exploring her steps forward after experiencing a stroke. In doing so, Ann expertly displays that what many think of as an event which leaves a patient a fraction of who they were and what they can accomplish, can instead be a grand restructuring of beauty filled perspectives and rediscovery of one's core self, where 'What seemed ordinary now is everything.' (Homecoming, Pg 11)

Knowing 'Unfulfilled dreams are like colors spilled on the ground' (Another Season, Pg 8), this accomplished poetess picked up her pen and wrote. First, as therapy, and then with defined purpose —to reclaim herself as a woman wordsmith and to assist others on their own journey through life changing experiences. Ann demonstrates through beautifully crafted poetry that even the hardest of circumstances can leave us even more determined, stronger in spirit, and clearly encouraged that 'Love will shape the day.' (Hope Will Shape Us, Pg 21)

~ C.J. Expression, poet & author

Table of Contents

Author's Note
Dedication
Foreword by C.J. Expression

Time and Place

The Unknown	2
No Words	3
Getting It Right	4
For Adam, The Doctor	5
Nights	6
December	7
Another Season	8
Before Sleep	10
Homecoming	11
October	12
A Pause	13
Lessons	14

Seasons of the Heart

My Morning Walk	16
June Morning	17
Winter Trees	18
Nancy Powell Petherick	19
Beside Us	20
Hope Will Shape Us	21

Stepping Forward

One Foot in Front of the Other	24
In Search of	25
Seeing is Believing	26
Still Life	27
Today	28
Listen	29
Perhaps	30
Night Writing	31
Pages	32
Secret Places	33
Silence	34
Time Passes	35
Failures	36
Lost and Found	37

About the Author

If I create from the heart nearly everything works.
~ Marc Chayal

Time and Place

The Unknown

Sun floods my desk. Hollow and weak,
I fall to the floor.

No movement, no strength,
this moment lasts forever.

A siren wails my name,
I want to stay home,

lock the bathroom door and cry.
Afraid of what I don't know.

No Words

> "Our innate capacity is the source of the
> most precious of our human qualities."
> ~ Dalai Lama

It was a late summer afternoon.
When the event struck, effortlessly,
when that space between light

and dark disappears, and a memory
is not yet a word. I thought of my good life,
when feet could lift like wings,

that I was who ever I was,
for a little while. Before the connection
was broken.

Day after day, I labor, Move forward,
knowing that this is the way
the world works.

Getting It Right

Fluorescent lights beam over my bed.
The walls are green, an ugly bedspread
covers me.

"Physical therapy three times a week,"
the neurologists said, agreement from
the interns in starched white coats.

I'm scared, I admit
I'll go a couple of times,
then I'll stop and quit.

Doctors checks my range of motion,
gives orders for an arduous plan
to ease the pain, regain control.

Bring me back from this dark, scary hole.
Sighs too deep for words, I crawl, push,
pedal and walk backward and forward.

Under a cream-fed moon every night,
I pray for morning to come. Strength
to get recovery right.

For Adam, The Doctor

> "People will forget what you said,
> people will forget what you did,
> people will never forget how
> you made them feel."
> ~ Maya Angelou

I remember the first time we met.
You said, "You don't know me from Adam,
but I am here for you."

You visited every day. Your voice
the color of wisdom. Your presence
an instrument of strength.

You know how sometimes you hear
something but just can't believe it?
How could a stranger speak words

that brought me to myself? To a place
I didn't know existed. We spoke daily,
never for very long.

It didn't matter; a few words here
and there from Adam was enough
to brighten the difficult day.

Lift me like a discarded flower
ready to burst, blossom
once again.

Lost and Found

Nights

Nights are stars, headlights on the wall,
glow of the clock, I am lost. Trying to find
my original place.

Where I can breathe with ease, and morning
meets me with welcome. Time to return,
retrace my steps, the heavy-hearted ones.

But how to find the path? Landscape
transformed, vanished. Memory is a mist
of rooms that remain closed.

The past gives way to a new day bursting
forth with hope, and the song I sing that
belongs to me.

December

Every day seems to be December.
I read the window for weather.

How can anything stay this way
for so long?

Months stretch where little
seems to change.

I do what I am told to do.
In and out of places I've

never seen before. The location
does not change my value.

The journey means nothing.
Can't anyone see that I am someone?

What matters is "I am here, I am here."
A miracle, even a small one, is welcomed.

Another Season

Another good summer gone,
and me another season older,

September comes quickly. The smell of
burning leaves lingers.

Three o'clock after-school bus run rubs
the sidewalk with shadows of trees.

Wind tilts slowly, days thin and pale.
Unfulfilled dreams are like colors spilled on the ground.

Is this how it begins?
Alone and not alone?

Where one plus one equals everything.
Forgetting where you are and what's to come.

So I step forward and say to the wind,
I am here for a reason.

Ann Falcone Shalaski

You can never go home again,
But the truth is you can never leave home,
so it's alright.

~ Maya Angelou

Before Sleep

I am homesick this afternoon,
for the evening light that rises
beyond the trees.

The way the little willows bend,
and tilt, reach for the ground.
How twilight splashes color

on the front walk. Evening looming.
Empty feelings fill my thoughts,
the loss of childhood, fleeting years.

Those poignant moments of memory,
almost too vague to recall. I catch,
hold them close.

As the sky, now dark October blue,
swirls, disappears from sight like the pull
on my blanket covering me before sleep.

Homecoming

I long to feel the sun on my face.
What seemed ordinary now is
everything.

See my purple iris bloom,
and the miniature roses
go silent at dusk.

Sit in my maple rocker
as the day fills with
bubbly songs of welcome.

Savor my homecoming where time takes
shape and a woman feels beyond
the comprehension of men

October

September has come and gone
with little to say except everything
that lives past summer doesn't die.

There is hope in the leaves first turning,
now fringed gold and crimson. Hands
reaching out to a curtain blue sky.

Winter will take what it will from the heat,
year after year in the shortened days –
as if stolen and never reclaimed.

As we age, we take seasons and hold them
in the twilight of memory where it lingers
and drops through our fingers.

Each year we grip tighter and tighter,
and see the faces of loved ones melt,
knowing our story hasn't begun.

A Pause

I look out the window,
watch leaves falling, wondering…

do trees remember a branches
green growth like we do?

Do breezes cry after ripping
balloons from a child's hand?

Perhaps it is the still before the fall.
A pause between breaths.

God's grace after the blessing.

Lessons

Winter comes. Empty snow-white streets
look glum.
The earth moves on.

Freezing gusts of wind whip through houses.
There's a glow inside.

Porches are dark. Tall oak trees disappear
in swirls of snow.

The earth moves on.
Winter is like a ring
with a single key. Cold sinks through my gloves.

My hands are numb. Words become a breath.
The earth moves on.

Morning opens like an old book.
Sometimes the lessons are quiet.

Poetry is when an emotion
has found its thought and the
thought has found words

~ Robert Frost

Seasons of the Heart

My Morning Walk

My morning walk brings me past
a silent white house.
Lone porch light left on.

Neighbors say the owner is away.
She's gone to rest, to get well.
Her heart beats too fast,

or maybe it's too slow.
She's lost her taste for living,
for friends and yard sales,

for talking and listening.
There is no one to care for,
no dinner to fix, and no one calls.

What will it take to mend a heart?
Or adjust the heart's rhythm
so it's strong, sure, steady as a radio beacon?

I see signs of welcome everywhere.
Last night's rain resurrected the impatiens.
They burst, flavoring the air.

Slight breeze ruffles the morning paper
by the front door proclaiming
life is good.

June Morning

There's dew on the morning grass.
A golden sun lounges
on the horizon.

I plant flowers in my garden,
not far from the house,
except instead of flowers

they became trees. And the house
became a clock, tilted slightly right.
Still, I was happy.

This was a good sign, more than
I hoped for. There are some who say,
I just don't understand.

But I see beauty in the trees,
faces of family long-gone,
and even my own.

When dawn spills over the roof every day,
I'm struck by the morning glories,
giving *thanks.*

Winter Trees

A closed heart can't greet a winter sky.
Sycamore and oak, reach for the sky
to offer praise – born from all the rooted

years of bearing the sky's weight.
Some nights an open heart is filled with
spaces between stars the mind can't grasp.

Winter trees praise no flags, no denominations,
they owe allegiance to the soil. Drop their seeds,
and make homes reaching toward heaven.

Ann Falcone Shalaski

Nancy Powell Petherick

> "Many people walk in and out of your
> life, but only true friends will leave
> a footprint in your heart."
> ~ Eleanor Roosevelt

Sorrow, an unrelenting ache, moves across our bodies.
Finds a home in every nook and crevice.
Pools in the bottom of our hearts.

Yet we continue to live. Continue to face
a brand-new day without her.
Yellow morning light breaks across the table,

missing one setting. Missing Nancy.
Brave and quiet, folded into sleep,
she passed.

Afternoon sun thin and pale,
balanced at her window.
How do we live without our friend?

Without feeling lost? Uncomplaining
as she was. And why is it not yesterday
when everything was right?

Before the final soft stir of silence
swept her away. Changed everything.
A change that is the same as sadness.

Beside Us

> "If I had a flower for every time
> I thought of you, I could walk
> through my garden forever."
> ~ Alfred Tennyson

The dead sit beside us,
and listen as we tell stories.

They are able to come and go.
Yet we continue to invite them in.

Retelling tales of summers past.
Vacations at the shore.

The Christmas dinners at grandma's.
Those precious memories linger.

We are blessed to have the dead
among us.

Already knowing what we
long to tell them.

Hope Will Shape Us

There is hope for the fading year.
Hope that next year will be better.
Blue birds will clatter in the wind,

cardinals alive with color.
You'll take me to the very spot
we picnicked many years ago.

I'll touch the freckles on your face,
search your gray eyes that ask so much.
Stir me in ways I've never known.

Love will shape the day.

Start by doing what is necessary,
then what is possible,
and suddenly you are doing
the impossible.

~ Saint Francis of Assisi

Stepping Forward

One Foot in Front of the Other

Memory is like a hammer,
a rope binding your wrists.

It turns its back on a dark place,
the details hide themselves

somewhere inside me.
Things I knew well,

I barely notice.
When I ask myself, about myself,

the light is so dim,
I cannot see.

Still, I take each step,
one foot in front of the other.

Ann Falcone Shalaski

In Search of...

I'm not sure when it happened,
but like Alice, I went down a
rabbit hole.

Hoping to find the girl in blue jeans,
curly brown hair, silver studs in her ears,
and a party smile.

But, like a star falling from the sky,
in red sneakers and yoga pants,
I thought, really!

I'm different now. I need to be fixed.
I'm not like the others.
I've lost me.

If I look long enough, maybe I will find
myself. I realized that the rabbit hole
mirrors every thing we live without.

That no dream is complete unless we can
see ourselves. So I'll strut my stuff,
sing, shout. Be the who I am.

Because to face the truth,
is to become beautiful.

Seeing is Believing

Everything I see is true.
Time has slipped through my fingers
like water in an open faucet.

Pretty pink blush on my cheeks
replaced now, with age spots.
Laugh-lines are crow's feet.

Osteoporosis looms, hip replacement
scheduled. No six-inch stilettos in my
closet. Orthopedic shoes

on the shelf to each the pain in my feet.
Cataracts cloud my landscape.
Morning sky, the color of gray-flannel.

There's no going back to things
that once were. I am what I am,
and I'll stop day dreaming

in this narrow world. Flaws can turn to gold.
Like a stain-glass window, catching sunlight,
I'll shine, I'll just shine!

Still Life

Morning slips simply in the front door.
I am at peace with the quiet shift of passing
from one space to another.

Today weighs heavy with the absence of presence.
In this moment of reflection there are rooms
that remain closed.

I feel it being painted without me.
I am missing from this glint
on the surface of life.

The sky was deeper blue then.
Clouds were cathedral-like.
Water rushed over rocks with effervescence.

Nothing is as it was.
I look for you everywhere and never
find the two of us together.

Today

Today I have learned
that you are never
too old to learn.

That the most important
person listening is
yourself.

I have learned that the leaves
of autumn that fall and are
swept away, do so without remorse.

For they, like men,
must make way for new
generations.

I have learned that today is ours,
our hopes, and our dreams.
That we are a part of life.

Today I have learned that
one is never too old
to learn.

Ann Falcone Shalaski

Listen

The pen called my name – poetry woke me
from a deep sleep. On a blank page,
I scratched out diamonds like wildflowers

beneath a pavement that remembers
how the sun felt. I'm miles away now,
on a journey of a wordsmith.

I jot notes, fly through blue-lines sheets
of pages. Listening to words.

Perhaps

I had an idea battering around
in my head. It turned into a bird –
the way a poem appears and

startles me. I'd like to be a bird next time.
Birds don't need to learn to love the world.
They can enter gray, dark skies.

Perhaps I'll be a shiny seal.
One who breaks the surface with news
of a deeper life.

The way I hope to come back as a poem
that surfaces again, and again.
Glistening.

Night Writing

Just when I think my words
are as dry as the paper I scratch,

that I'll never have another
illuminating thought,

words filter through the blinds.
Whisper in my ear.

When I think my brain is silenced,
shuttered like a summer cottage.

Words build, begging to be framed.
When I believe I'm the star writer

of the mundane, brilliant words wake
me. Remind me that poetry

is written in the middle of the night,
listening to the magic of words.

Pages

With a poem in mind,
I look for blank spaces
on the pages of my notebook.

At times, I think the beauty
of words is in the flowing
of thoughts,

the slivers of silver spreading
sunlight on water, or the slow
slips of rain that slide into nothing

as though they had been called.

Ann Falcone Shalaski

Secret Places

My mind is a walled room,
with high windows overlooking
the river, a moon that rises,

and quickly falls away. It's my secret place.
A sanctuary where anything is possible.
Maybe tomorrow, I'll send word

of my private world. Until then,
comfort comes from things
as simple as stone.

Peace, too faint to ignore,
clearly defines my future.

Silence

I lose myself in silence,
like a fugitive from the world.
Reflect on what moves,

leaves fluttering on the walk,
wind tearing holes in the sky,
breath exhaled on my pillow.

A world of silence,
one motion, one voice.
Silence, where no one is alone.

Time Passes

It is early. A bird flies deep
into the sky. The sun so new
it weaves hair-thin rays

through shadows. This hush
of morning in my room is my story –
the trees my only company.

I take time to breathe in this hour,
and ask for time to take me where
it will.

Failures

Words fail because we believe
there is an explanation for everything.

Numbers fail when we believe love
can be measured.

Science fails when we believe that
the infinite can be explained.

Art fails when we believe beauty
is a limited commodity.

Belief fails every time we try to
avoid what we don't know.

Lost and Found

I lost out,
      I found out.

I lost time,
      I found myself.

I lost the key,
      I found the door.

I lost my train of thought,
      I found the right words.

I lost a dear friend,
      I found an old flame.

I lost my business,
      I found my calling.

I lost faith,
      I found God.

I lost sleep,
      I found peace.

I lost my way,
      I found direction.

I lost patience,
      I found hope.

Ann Falcone Shalaski

Meet Your Poet

Ann Falcone Shalaski is an award-winning poet, born and raised in Connecticut. Her prose and poetry have appeared in *Keeper of the Stories, A Guide to Writing Family Stories, The Comstock Review, The Poet's Domain, The Meridian Anthology of Contemporary Poetry, First Literary Review – East* among many others.

Ann is past President of the advisory council for Christopher Newport University's Writers' Conference, and an Executive Director of the Poetry Society of Virginia.

She conducts writing workshops, judges contests and mentors aspiring writers.

Colophon

Wider Perspectives Publishing regrets to have to announce that the ongoing Colophon page, used to tout artists published in books from WPP, has to be reworked. This is due to the growing library of fine writers coming out of, or even into, the Hampton Roads area of Virginia.

Samantha Casey
Donna Burnett-Robinson
Faith Griffin
Se'Mon-Michelle Rosser
Lisa M. Kendrick
Cassandra IsFree
Nich (Nicholis Williams)
Samantha Geovjian Clarke
Natalie Morison-Uzzle
Gus Woodward II
Patsy Bickerstaff
Edith Blake
Jack Cassada
Dezz
Daniel Garwood
Jada Hollingsworth
Tabetha Moon House
Travis Hailes- Virgo, thePoet
Nick Marickovich
Grey Hues
Rivers Raye
Madeline Garcia
Chichi Iwuorie
Symay Rhodes
Tanya Cunningham
   (Scientific Eve)
Terra Leigh
Raymond M. Simmons
Samantha Borders-Shoemaker

Taz Weysweete'
Jade Leonard
Darean Polk
Bobby K. (The Poor Man's Poet)
J. Scott Wilson (Teech!)
Charles Wilson
Gloria Darlene Mann
Neil Spirtas
Jorge Mendez & JT Williams
Sarah Eileen Williams
Stephanie Diana (Noftz)
Shanya – Lady S.
Jason Brown (Drk Mtr)
Ken Sutton
Kailyn Rae Sasso
Crickyt J. Expression

Crystal Nolen
Catherine TL Hodges
Kent Knowlton
Maria April C.

the Hampton Roads
   Artistic Collective (757
   Perspectives) &
The Poet's Domain
are all WPP literary journals in cooperation with Scientific Eve or Live Wire Press

Check for those artists on FaceBook, Instagram, the Virginia Poetry Online channel on YouTube, and other social media.

Ann Falcone Shalaski

Made in the USA
Middletown, DE
01 April 2025